Breast Cancer And Me

Dealing With Your State Of Mind

Vanessa Knowles

Book Cover Designed By EvoWorld Design

www.evoworldent.com/

Published By Pataskity Publishing Company

Pataskity Publishing (USA) LLC.

www.Pataskitypublishing.com

Copyright © 2021. All rights reserved. No portion of this book may be reproduced mechanically, electronically, or by any other means, including photocopying, without the author's written permission. It is illegal to copy this book, post it on a website, or distribute it by any other means without permission from the author.

This Book Is In Memory Of

My Mom,

My Biggest Supporter,

Lady Willie Mae Richmond.

Table of Contents

About Vanessa Brown-Knowles 1

Get On Your Knees And Pray 3
    Taking Charge Of Your Health 3

Chapter 1: 8
    The Battle Is Not Yours 8
    Discovering Faith During The Battle 8
    The Initial Shock 16
    The Day My Life Changed Forever 16

Chapter 3: 26
    If You Can't Tell It, Let Me Tell It 26
    Early Detection Saves Lives 26

Chapter 4 35
    The God That I Sang About
    Call Him When You Are Sick 35

Chapter 5: 51
    You Can Make It 51
    Play The Hand That You Are Dealt 51

Chapter 6: 61
Wait On The Lord To Move 61
The State of Mind.. 61

Chapter 7: 66
Have A Little Talk With Jesus............................. 66
He Is Strong When You Are Weak 66

Chapter 8: 71
God Kept His Arms Around Me 71
Pulling Me Through... 71

Chapter 9: 74
God Can Do It... 74
This Too Shall Pass.. 74

Chapter 10 82
How We Made It 82
Trusting And Believing 82

About Vanessa Brown-Knowles

Ms. Vanessa Brown- Knowles was born and raised in Memphis, Tennessee, to the late Willie Mae (Brown) Richmond. Knowles is the oldest of five children. Even as a child, it was always instilled in Vanessa to put God first in everything she does. She learned early that God, our Father, is a rewarder of those who diligently seek him, so that is what she found herself doing.

Vanessa found herself singing quartet in the late 70's while she was yet a teenager under the direction of her mom. In Memphis, a female gospel quartet was formed by her mother, Willie Mae, and named by their pastor. She is now the only original still singing in the group. Knowles has been fortunate to sing with three generations.

In 2002, Vanessa was diagnosed with Stage Two Breast Cancer, which led to her having both chemotherapy and radiation therapy treatment. In April of 2003, she received the report that the cancer was gone. Knowles then decided to dedicate the rest of her life to supporting others who were actively battling breast cancer and educating both men and women on the importance of annual exams. In 2017, after forty years of singing, The Brown

Singers decided to shift from celebrating their Homecoming Weekend into using the platform they gained over the years to support Vanessa as she launched Survivor Fest. A part of the proceeds of Survivor Fest are used to bless people who are actively battling cancer.

For several years, Knowles has been sharing her story with her family, friends, and anyone who may come in contact with her. Upon surviving Breast Cancer for eighteen years, she is elated to share her story as a testimony of God's grace. Knowles is the author of **Breast Cancer And Me**. Her mission is always to let others know that it is not over until God says it is over despite their situation or circumstances!

Vanessa Knowles resides in her hometown of Memphis, TN. She is the mother of two beautiful children, Lisa, and Devyn, whom she cherishes. Vanessa has dedicated her life to loving family, and spending time spoiling her beautiful grandchildren. Because of God's miraculous healing power, Vanessa has also devoted her time to empowering, educating, and supporting every cancer patient by letting them know that they, too, will survive.

Get On Your Knees And Pray
Taking Charge Of Your Health

"Father, thank You for working Your eternal glory in me. I cast my cares on You today, knowing that my trials and troubles are temporary. Thank You for Your eternal blessing on my life today, and for leading me into victory in Jesus' name, Amen."

Ms. Vanessa Brown-Knowles
18 Year Survivor

The purpose of **Breast Cancer And Me** is to strengthen you for the process of SURVIVING! Whatever you go through in life, never lose HOPE or sight of God. Always know that PRAYER is the key to unlock any door. You can learn how to SURVIVE the storms of life as it is a lifelong lesson that applies to any circumstance, and not just cancer. In times like these, please keep a positive attitude. I know at this time you may be overwhelmed and disgusted because of how things are going for you, and sometimes you cannot even pray. This is the time to grab a prayer partner, someone who you know and trust to pray for you and with you. Surround yourself with family, church family and friends. Prayer is especially important to gain your strength and your state of mind. You may be having a pity party, but this is the time you need a support system. You need someone who you can call on to pray. Prayer makes all the difference. Grab a minister or someone who you trust to get a prayer through on your behalf. Stay away from negative people who carry negative spirits. Be around positive people.

Do not isolate yourself as you may feel like you sharing your burdens are a bother to others. If you need help fighting your thoughts or even the enemy, reach out to someone for prayer. Do not isolate yourself. Instead, surround yourself with friends and family. Remember, laughter is good for the soul. A song that often blesses me is, "*Lord, If You Guide Me, I Will Not Go Wrong.*" YES, the flesh gets weak. Surviving cancer can feel like a catastrophe, and this is "breathtaking" resulting in feelings of shock and disbelief! This new wave will leave anyone questioning God. Take a moment, breathe in and then breathe out. Reflect on God's grace (try to smile at a memory). If you seek God's guidance, he will not lead you in the wrong direction. It is not "easy," but you can have victory over your situation.

Psalm 29:11 allows us to know of God being our biggest support system, "The LORD will give STRENGTH to YOU, the LORD will bless YOU with PEACE." Did you know that your fight did not just begin? You have fought and won since your birth SURVIVING and LIVING in water in your mother's womb, then bursting into life and breathing God's air. The first miracle that God performed was birthing you (happy moment, huh)! Because you did not drown is evident that you are a miracle. God healing you is just another one of his miraculous acts.

Do not dwell on thinking negatively during times that are the most challenging. You may ask, *"What to ask God for during some of the darkest moments in our lives?"* It is especially important to know to ask God for peace of mind in the midst of your storm. I often say to God, *"Ain't nothing I can do with this, but you can. Whatever is going on in my body, my mind, and even my life, I give it to you."* Remember, no doctor can do what God can do. Pray for the doctors. Pray for everyone who has to make decisions about your health. Whenever you pray, you must believe that God hears you. Psalm 120:1 states, "I called on the Lord in my distress, and he answered me." We must have faith and believe that God hears us. What God did then, he can do it again. If he did it for me, he could do it for you. I encourage you to get a relationship with God. Get him on your mind. Trust him in whatever place you are in, in your life, and he will keep you.

I thank God that he has blessed us to be able to gain knowledge through various resources now more than ever. Today much more resources are offered than in past years. We can become knowledgeable about our health. Attending to our health is important. Males and females should be watchful of irregular lumps that may come in the breast or chest. Whenever it is said that one is at high risk of getting breast cancer, this is to say that the person has a higher probability of getting breast cancer due to certain factors such as family history, genetic traits or mutation. One of the most frequent signs of breast cancer is lumps in the breast.

Although lumpy breasts can help detect breast cancer, this is not always an indication of breast cancer. For example, fatty tissues may often feel like lumps and are referred to as non-dense breast tissue, which means that your breast may be almost entirely fatty. Because you have lumps or fatty tissues does not mean that you have breast cancer. Don't panic! Fatty tissues are not always cancerous.

All women who are at forty years of age should have a yearly mammogram. If you have any irregular experiences such as nipple discharge, breast pain, nipple turning inward, swelling of part of the breast, or dimpling, you should have your mammogram earlier. Once you get your annual mammogram, it will make you aware of what is going on in your body. I always say to others, *"It is better to know than to not know. Again, you need to be scared not to go to the doctor for a regular complete physical examination. Make sure you are aware of what is going on in your body, and know that you are never alone."*

Chapter 1:
The Battle Is Not Yours
Discovering Faith During The Battle

The foundation I grew up on was one built by parents who loved the Lord. I grew up in the church. I was blessed to have the opportunity of knowing about Jesus at an early age. My mother knew and loved the Lord. She was a Gospel singer. Since my biological father, Joseph Brown passed away when I was only five years old, God placed my father, London Joe Richmond in my life. My father is a pastor, and my mother was the first lady. Because of who my parents were, I went to church all the time. I went when I wanted to go and when I did not want to go.

Attending church often as a child had many benefits. One of the benefits is that I learned about Jesus Christ at an early age. God does not look for perfection in families, but he does sustain families who love him and teach their children about him. There are no perfect families because there are no perfect people. However, growing up in a Christian home provided me the opportunity to learn about faith in God. The faith I learned about as a child became essential for my life. Because my foundation was built on knowing and having a personal relationship with Jesus Christ, I grew strong in my faith. In life, we all have storms that will come.

One may ask, "*How will we be prepared to overcome and endure the test of life?*" For me, even as a little child, God knew the obstacles I would encounter during my adult life, which I never saw as a child. There is an importance of learning about who Jesus is at an early age. I found out when I was young that similar to my mother, music is my ministry.

I loved music at a very young age. I was the choir director in school. Singing always took me somewhere else. Singing makes me feel as if I am in a different place, and it alters my state of mind. Singing increases my faith. I have always felt a closer connection to God whenever I sing Gospel music. As I grew older and became of age, singing became more than a hobby; it became my ministry. From my experiences as a child, I learned that we could make it if we trust in Jesus despite what life brings. People handle situations differently. Although my mom would sing while sweeping, I would sing while going through my storm. Singing while going through the storm kept me going and being the best that I can be with my mother by my side and always praying.

One of my favorite memories of my mother is how she would hang pictures of the family on the walls. She would look up at the pictures on the wall, touch the picture, and pray. She was a prayer warrior. I heard her many of days singing while she was sweeping. If there was ever a problem she encountered, the family rarely knew of it because she would be sweeping, cleaning, and singing. Thus, I learned early on through my mom's experiences that we can praise and worship our way through life's toughest moments. Being diagnosed with breast cancer would eventually become a tough moment for me, but I knew the power of prayer and praise. I knew what faith felt like as it grew inside of me.

Over the years, as I grew from a child to a young lady, and from a young lady to a woman, I realized that my mother's relationship with God was most special because she had faith in God. My mother overcame her darkest moments in life because her faith shined as a light in her, and through her into the lives of her children and family. I learned from my mother, and she would always talk about that small still voice. I grew in faith. I grew because my mother's faith transpired into my life as I was able to lean on her during my toughest moments. She became a prayer partner as she was a prayer warrior. She was there for me every step of the way. Although I have battled with breast cancer, I have learned that faith can get us through anything. Learning how to cope with breast cancer is like learning to cope with the many challenges that life brings. Whenever we find ourselves in dark moments, we still have to fight the battle! We cannot give up. For example, you cannot just lay down and roll over. I could not just roll over, wallow, or just feel sorry for myself. Somehow, I had to get up and dust myself off. I had to pick myself up and get ready for the fight. Remember, when you fall down, you have to take a deep breath. Inhale, exhale, and calm down. Then, pick yourself up and fight to survive. Rather if it is any type of cancer, sickness, or life's battles, we must fight to win.

You may ask, *"How do I fight the battle?"* 2nd Chronicles 32:7-8, "Be strong and courageous, be not afraid nor dismayed for the King of Assyria, nor for all the multitude that is with him: for there be more with us than with him: With him is an arm of flesh; but with us is the Lord our God to help us, and to fight our battles. And the people rested themselves upon the words of Hezekiah King of Judah." We all can become weary, but we should have faith in the Lord when we feel most weary. Faith is what we believe, and we have to trust that the situation will get better. God gives us all a measurement of faith. The measurement of your faith may not be the same as the measurement of my faith. When I think of faith, I think of a job that I will get paid on eventually. Although you do not see the money because you are working in advance, you know you will get paid. The Bible defined faith; Hebrews 11:1 teaches, "Now faith is the substance of things hoped for, the evidence of things not seen."

Faith is believing that God will do it even if you cannot see the end. Faith is believing that God will provide water even if you cannot see its streams. Faith is believing that God will lead you past the red sea even if you cannot see a ship. Having faith in God is believing that God will take you to the palace even if you are still in the prison. Having faith in God is trusting him for healing, even if we have an illness. Faith is trusting that God will do what is best not only when we understand but also when we do not understand God's choices. The Bible often teaches us about the measurement of faith. In Matthew 17:20, Jesus teaches his disciples about the measurement of faith one should have, "Jesus said: Verily I say unto you, if ye have faith as a grain of mustard seed, ye shall say unto this mountain, remove hence to yonder place, and it shall remove, and **nothing shall be impossible unto you**." This mountain for me was breast cancer.

We should not only learn to have faith in the Lord but also recognize that without faith, it is impossible to please God. The scripture teaches in Hebrews 11:6, "But without faith, it is impossible to please him, for he that cometh must believe that he is, and he is the rewarder of them that diligently seek him." Having faith in God makes God happy. It shows that you believe in him. If we trust and have faith, we will always reap the reward. Having faith in God is not a "what will be, will be" attitude. Instead, having faith in God is saying, *"I know He will get me through this."* It is absolute and total confidence in God. It is having no plan B. We fall down, but we have to get back up, believing that God will pull us through.

Faith in God is strength and not weakness. The psalmist says in the book of Psalm 20:7, "Some trust in chariots and some in horses, but we trust in the name of the Lord our God." Faith is not trusting in your intellect or strength but trusting entirely on God and believing that he will do it. In further detail, many people had advice for me when I was diagnosed with breast cancer. Eighteen years ago, no one talked a lot about breast cancer, lumpectomies, or mastectomies. I could not listen to the negative things that people said when I was diagnosed with breast cancer. I had to tune out so many things that I heard, so I could listen to what Jesus Christ was speaking to me and learn how to trust him.

Like many survivors before me, I was in awe because of their strength and what they had to endure. While I had seen their glory, I did not know their story. Now I know that people I have met who survived tough times had to lean on God. The Bible states in Romans 10:17, "So, then faith cometh by hearing, and hearing by the word of God." What I have endured made me wiser, stronger, and built my faith over time. Faith connected me to Jesus Christ, and I learned to trust him while dealing with breast cancer. I have grown in faith over a period of time.

PERSONAL NOTE: GOD GOT ME AND HE GOT YOU TOO! If you are worried, down, and out, pray to gain faith. If you can get you a little faith, just one scripture and a song in your heart, it will help you to get through whatever battles you go through in life. Remember to cast all of your cares on the Lord. He will see you through!

Recap: Never fail to see your future, and yes, your future is bright! Take a deep breath. Tell yourself, "*This battle belongs to the Lord.*" You do not have to fight alone. You have a higher power in you which is Jesus Christ.

Chapter 2:

The Initial Shock
The Day My Life Changed Forever

In February of 2002, I woke up one morning, and my breast was so sore under my arms on both sides. After examining myself one evening in the shower, I felt a knot on my breasts under both of my lower armpits. I went on with my day and did not worry much about it because I knew that sometimes I had previously experienced small little knots under my arms, but they never lasted for long. I thought to myself, "*It may not be much. Maybe these knots are coming from the deodorant, and they will soon go away.*"

The next day, the knots were still there underneath my armpits. I began to think and ask myself, "*What could this be?*" In my inner voice, I said, "*Oh well, this would soon probably go away too.*" One week passed, and the knots were still there. It was time for my menstrual cycle. And sometimes, my breasts get tender around this time of the month. Because of this, I thought to myself, "*I will just wait until my menstrual cycle begins and ends. If the knots are still there, I would call my OBGYN doctor.*" I knew that all lumps are not cancerous, and sometimes a woman's breast can become tender even during her menstrual cycle. However, my menstrual cycle ended. I thought to myself, "*Oh, Lord, these lumps are still here! Let me call my doctor.*"

Initially, I visited Dr. Allen, my OBGYN. Dr. Allen examined me and felt a lump in both of my breasts because both lumps were still there. At that point, Dr. Allen referred me to Dr. Fuller for an ultrasound. During that time, my OBGYN was not doing ultrasounds in her office.

Scheduling time between each appointment was always a few weeks. After Dr. Fuller completed the ultrasound, he then sent the ultrasound results back to Dr. Allen. Upon Dr. Allen reviewing the ultrasound results, she said to me, "*Abnormal tissues are present, but they could be just fatty tissues; however, I am now referring you to see Dr. Monroe, a breast specialist for further examination such as a biopsy.*"

It took a few more weeks for me to get an appointment. I waited to have a biopsy. I had no idea about what a biopsy was because I had never experienced this in prior years. I had no thoughts about me having cancer; I had not thought about it at all. I had no idea or pre-notion of what the breast clinic doctor was going to tell me.

While Dr. Monroe was scheduled to do a Biopsy, she also did a mammogram and an ultrasound. A biopsy is when a small amount of tissues from the lump are removed and examined under a microscope to see if cancer is present. My biopsy was done in the doctor's office, and it was a same-day procedure. I had to recover quickly from having the biopsy due to me attending my mother's birthday dinner in two hours once I got home on that day. The birthday dinner took my mind off of everything that went on earlier that day.

If you are having any type of biopsy, I would suggest that you take someone with you. Just remember that because your doctor orders a biopsy does not mean that you have cancer. Following a biopsy, be prepared to rest for the remaining of the day. It is best to rest prior to resuming your usual activities. I had the biopsy, not thinking or even aware that the phone call I was anticipating a few days later would be life changing. I was expecting my doctor to call me, but I surely wasn't expecting the results that I was given.

On the day I received a life-changing phone call, I am so glad that my mother was at my house. She and I were just sitting around, enjoying each other's company. My doctor called from The Breast Clinic. She called and said, "*Is anybody there with you?*" I said, "*Yes, my mom is here with me.*" She said, "*Well, normally we would have you come into the office, but since your mom is there with you, I am going to tell you over the phone. We did find cancer.*" I was blown away. Those words took me for an initial shock. I had to absorb what she had just told me. At that moment, I was in disbelief. This type of news took time for me to accept, and I had to prepare my mind for what I was about to go through the big words, BREAST CANCER. Y'all, this was a moment that I will never, ever forget! I had to call on God to renew my mind and my strength. The scripture states in Isaiah 41:10, "Fear thou not; for I am with thee: be not dismayed; for I am thy

God: I will strengthen thee; yea, I will help thee; yea, I will uphold thee with the right hand of my righteousness."

Whenever we hear the word CANCER, we wonder about the rest of our lives. Fear does appear. During this moment, my whole life flashed before my eyes. My children were young, and I was a single parent. I was devastated on this day. I began to cry! I thought to myself, "A*m I really hearing this? Am I hearing that I have cancer?*" With tears in eyes, my mom immediately consoled me. She said to me, *"We are going to get through this trusting God*, so try not to worry."

I thought of many things. I thought about my daughter and son, my whole family, singing in the group, and many more thoughts came to my mind. It seemed like someone was getting sick every five months, and I felt concerned about my life and my future. As I began to process the news, I started relying on songs. Every time I would think about what I was about to go through or experience, I would focus on a song that always got my state of mind on the man who made us. Just know that in the time of trouble, God is a very present help. I always enjoyed hearing my son, Devyn and my daughter, Lisa sing, "Take It To Jesus, He Will Make It Alright." Singing Gospel songs assured me that all of my cares were in God's hands. I kept thinking, "Jesus Is On The Main Line, Tell Him What You Want." I reflected on spiritual songs that we sang, such as: "God's Got Everything You Need," "Waymaker," and "You Can Make It," are just a few titles.

I was in a place of gloominess and a dark moment, but I thought about the man who made me. I said to God, "*I trust you. I sing all of these songs all of the time*; Now, *I must trust you in the place that I am in, and the battle starts in my mind.*" In other words, I had to stay focused on God. Whenever you are in this type of situation, you are going to have thoughts that will cause your faith to waiver. Every time you have those kinds of thoughts, you have to recondition your mind.

Proverbs 23:7, "As a man thinketh in his heart, so is he." My initial shock did not cause my faith to waiver because I knew that God was in total control. I had to recondition my mind. Recondition your mind for good thoughts. Tell yourself, *"I am going to live, laugh and enjoy each moment."* I have found out every moment counts.

The day that I received that phone call was the day that my life changed forever. Time immediately became an important factor. I had to take the time to absorb this news and regroup. It was most important for me to gather my thoughts and prepare to take charge of my health. Once I took all the time that I needed, I scheduled a time to meet with my doctor for she and I to talk about what she found, the biopsy being cancerous, and planning for the next steps.

The Bible says something so beautiful and profound in Proverbs 18:21, "The tongue has the power of life and death, and those who love it will eat its fruit." Philippians 2:5 states, "Let this mind be in you which was also in Christ Jesus." I would say to anyone who encounters this type of an experience to condition your mind and think on good thoughts.

This is to say that your words can either give life to situations or circumstances or take life from circumstances.

So, we have to be careful about our use of words. Always learn to be positive whenever you speak. Speak positively over your body, life, family, and your doctor even if you do not feel like it. You may not feel like saying beautiful words to yourself, but discipline yourself always to do it as an exercise.

Whatever you begin to say with your mouth, soon your body and your feelings will adjust to it. For example, if you feel depressed and unloved, look at a mirror, and say encouraging words to yourself. Call yourself well, healed, and whole. Whenever you do this, your feelings and emotions will adjust to the words you say.

Do not let your emotions or feelings rule you. If you are sick, tell yourself, *"I am healed."* If the enemy tries to deter you from believing that you can be whole, decree, *"I am coming out of this. I will win! I am well, and it is well!"* Whenever you are in a bad situation or things are not working out, just speak the word of God concerning that issue.

PERSONAL NOTE: GOD WILL MAKE A WAY. YOUR WHOLE FUTURE IS AHEAD OF YOU, SO KEEP

GOING! Problems and mountains have ears; they can hear. There is so much authority in you because you are a child of the King. Speak with that authority. Keep speaking! This builds faith within your heart, and it gives you hope and peace that this world cannot give you. There is an assurance that just comes on you whenever you speak the word of God, and you keep saying it. That is faith rising within you. Change will come, but you have to condition your mind to go with the change.

Some circumstances in life will knock you down, but you can get back up. I have been knocked down to the point where I could not wait to get to church. "*Lord, blink me in the church*" is what I would normally say to God because I needed to get to the church in a hurry. I needed to be in the room. I knew being in the church, it would give me a little more strength. I was in the place where I would go to sleep with the problems on my mind, and I would wake up with the same problems. I would ask myself, "*How am I going to get back up?*" I knew that I had to pray or even call someone to pray for me and with me to get back up.

Recap: Sometimes news can weigh heavy on your mind. A lot of times, we hold stuff in because we do not want to talk about it. In those moments, we need to reach out and get somebody in a hurry. It is important to always know the power of prayer. Reach out to someone who you trust to pray with and for you. Learning to pray is a life-long lesson. My experiences made me aware of many life-long lessons.

Being aware of your body is also a lifelong lesson. Regular self- examinations are especially important. Because early detection is the best protection, you should frequently examine your breast. I began to examine my breast once I noticed the pain and discomfort. Looking back at that time is when I learned the importance of checking my breast. Later, I learned that the best time to self-examine your breast is one week after your monthly cycle. Self- examination is important to ensure that lumps are detected early. Any signs of breast changes can be followed up by a mammogram.

Chapter 3:
If You Can't Tell It, Let Me Tell It
Early Detection Saves Lives

Finding Breast Cancer early can save your life just like it saved my life. You may ask, *"What is early detection?"* Early detection is going to the doctor at a minimum of once a year for a check-up. Early detection is making a commitment to learn and know your body. Whenever something looks irregular, do not take too long to go to the doctor.

While many times we are afraid to go to the doctor, we should be scared not to go. Going to check-ups frequently helps one to detect early if they have an illness or any disease. Research shows that early screening for any type of cancer reduces your risk of advancement by twenty- five to thirty percent or more. You would never have to live with the thought, *"What if?"* Detecting changes in your body early is a win/win situation. Do your best to stay healthy.

There are various reasons why many people avoid going to the doctor. Some people may feel that they cannot afford to go to the doctor, or that their lives are too busy with other demands, which prevents them from scheduling time to check on their health. Regardless of the reason, you may not visit the doctor, no one can afford not to go. There are many opportunities for uninsured people to go to the doctor and receive assistance going. My motto is, "*If you don't go, you will not know.*" Whenever breast cancer is detected and treated early, the chances of survival are very high. I am glad I detected the changes early on that my body was experiencing.

PERSONAL NOTE: GOD IS IN CONTROL. During the appointment after my biopsy, my doctor talked about the next steps, which were to have the lump removed. I had to have the mass removed. We discussed my surgery, which was to have a lumpectomy being scheduled for June 11. I guess Dr. Monroe saw the surprise look on my face and said to me, "*It is all in your state of mind how you deal with this situation.*" Dr. Monroe explained that I had a fifty, fifty chance of survival regardless of whether I had a lumpectomy or mastectomy. Dr. Monroe explained that a lumpectomy is when one has a mass removed (removal of the lump and the tissues around it) and that the mastectomy is removing the whole breast. Dr. Monroe recommended that I have a lumpectomy.

Most women survive breast cancer! There is a high percentage of women who are doing well even after five years of being diagnosed. Breast cancer is one of the most common types of cancer women may encounter in their lifetime. While it can occur at any age, the risk factors increase with age. Because of certain factors, some women may have a higher risk of getting breast cancer than others. Every woman needs to know about breast cancer and how to prevent it. Being educated about breast cancer not only helps to detect it earlier, but also save lives. Read and learn what you can do. The best defense is to discover breast cancer early, when it is small, has not spread, and is easy to treat. **PERSONAL NOTE: AGAIN, EARLY DETECTION CAN SAVE YOUR LIFE!**

After receiving my diagnosis, I had so much gratitude because of my support system. Having a good support system and healthy oriented relationships is essential to our endurance of the storms of life. For example, having someone whom you can depend on who can get a prayer through is essential. We often get so much information when going to the doctor. Too much information may cause one to feel overwhelmed. While I knew that God was with me, I also gained strength from my mother, family, and friends.

I am thankful for the support of my mother. My mom supported me through so many good days and bad times during my challenges with breast cancer. One day we were at a doctor's visit, and my doctor shared encouraging words. My mom said, "*Wow, I like her.*" My mom approved of Dr. Monroe because she picked up on her good spirit alongside her attentiveness to my health. It meant a lot to me to have my mother with me through the experiences, doctor visits, and just a prayer when I needed it.

I recall that on the day I had my surgery, as they scrolled me into the operating room, I said, "*Me and the Lord, we are about to go handle this."* At that point, I had been singing about the Lord for many years. I believed in God for a long time, so now is the time for me to trust him. Because I had a lumpectomy, the surgeon removed only the cancerous lump and the surrounding tissue. The breast usually retains its shape. The tissue margin is examined under a microscope. The doctors proceeded to test the lymph nodes under my armpits as well to see if they were cancerous. The results showed that the cancer had spread to some of my lymph nodes, which means that I had Stage II- B Carcinoma Breast Cancer (early-stage breast cancer), meaning breast cancer is growing, but it is still contained in the breast or it has only extended to the lymph nodes.

Once I had the lymph nodes removed, I later had Lymphedema. I visited my doctor, and I had therapy on my arm and was later given a compression arm sleeve to keep the swelling down. Lymphedema is abnormal swelling that can develop in the arm as a side effect of breast cancer surgery. Lymphedema can appear in some people within months or even years after treatment ends. Therefore, you should always have any IVs or blood drawn on the opposite side from which breast cancer was removed. It is best not to do any heavy lifting on that side. Any swelling or pain should be checked by a health care provider right away.

Some people may have severe swelling, with the infected arm being seven inches larger than the other arm. Other symptoms may include heaviness or tightness in the chest or armpit area, aching or new pain in the arm, swelling in the hands, and weakening in the arms. Therefore, you should not lift anything with the affected side to prevent Lymphedema. If you notice any health changes, see a healthcare professional right away.

My children and family often look at me for being strong. My motto is, "*Keep your mind on the prize. The one who made you. His name is Jesus.*" Dealing with life's situations is just like playing cards. I will play the hand I'm dealt, and I will play to win, meaning I have to trust in God every step of the way. You have to give it all you got by casting every one of your cares on the Lord and knowing that he is in charge. The hand that you are dealt when dealing with life is not always good. You have to choose to not dwell on the negative and focus on the positive. Try not to allow your mind to dwell on your diagnosis. Instead, think about your healing. Do not allow your condition to cause you to feel like the situation will last forever. Do not allow your condition cause you to forfeit your future. All of the steps toward healing are temporary, and none are permanent. Even when it seems darkest, the sun will shine again. There are millions of breast cancer survivors. Smile!

Referring to Biblical scriptures always encouraged me. Do you recall the Biblical story about Lazarus? Although Lazarus was a follower of Jesus, he became ill. His sisters knew that Jesus loved Lazarus, so they sent messages to Jesus to come and save their brother from dying. Jesus did not come immediately. Can you imagine the disappointment they must have felt, in their hearts, the pain they must have felt when Jesus did not show up? They waited. They must have told their sick brother not to worry that Jesus would be here soon, but Jesus came four days later. He came after Lazarus' death, and by then, Lazarus had already been buried. Martha must have asked, "*Why did you come? He is already gone. There is no hope.*"

Jesus went on and performed a miracle that is still marveling to this day. He called Lazarus from the grave; a man buried for four days. Lazarus stood up and came out of the tomb, and the crowd that was there was amazed to see a man they had already signed off as dead walk towards them. Jesus spoke words to Lazarus' body, and it repaired itself. He spoke to Lazarus' cold heart, and it received life, and many marveled and turned to go to Jesus. God is never late. Let me tell you why this is such a powerful story! If God can call Lazarus back to life, don't you think he can heal you from cancer? Smile! That gave me a happy moment, huh? Keep your state of mind, tuned in to God's plans for your life.

The Bible teaches us in the Book of 2nd Peter 3:9, "The Lord is not slow in keeping his promise, as some understand slowness. Instead, he is patient with you." Remember that the doctors do the cutting, but God does the healing. The story of Lazarus reminds us that God may not have come when we wanted him to, but God is always on time.

Again, please pay attention to your body. Although I discovered breast cancer during stage two, by getting yearly mammograms, breast cancer can be discovered at stage zero. If you do not go to the doctor, you will not know what is going on with your body.

Recap: **BELIEVE AND BE PATIENT.** As you go through your journey, Proverbs 3:5-6 states, "Trust in the LORD with all thine heart; and lean not unto thine own understanding. In all thy ways acknowledge him, and he will direct your paths." There may be days when you may feel tired and want to give up. There may be days when you may feel down and as if you just do not want to fight through this process anymore. I say to you, *"Trust and wait on the Lord. Believe and be patient."*

Early detection can save your life! Mammograms are important to you learning and knowing your status. Starting at the age of forty, women should have mammograms yearly; however, if there is a history of breast cancer or any type of cancer in your family, you are at a higher risk.

Chapter 4
The God That I Sang About
Call Him When You Are Sick

Now that Dr. Monroe had removed the cancer from my breast and the lymph nodes, I was very sore from this surgery and needed to rest. The surgical operation was outpatient. Breast tissues are very tender. There was discomfort and some common swelling. I was also given pain pills. I was told to avoid heavy lifting, pushing, and pulling. I had to sleep on my back for a while, and of course, keep the bandages dry and clean. It took me four to six weeks to heal from this surgery. I had to prepare and let the healing begin.

There are several things you may experience after breast cancer is removed. Some people may experience drainage. Drainage occurs whenever fluid is present after tissue and muscle are separated. The fluid is the raw surface that leaks. Because the doctors want the fluid to come out, thin tubes are inserted into one's chest or underneath the arm to drain excess fluid. These tubes are called drains. The drain will only remain in the chest for a few days. Experiences that you may encounter will vary depending upon what your doctor decides.

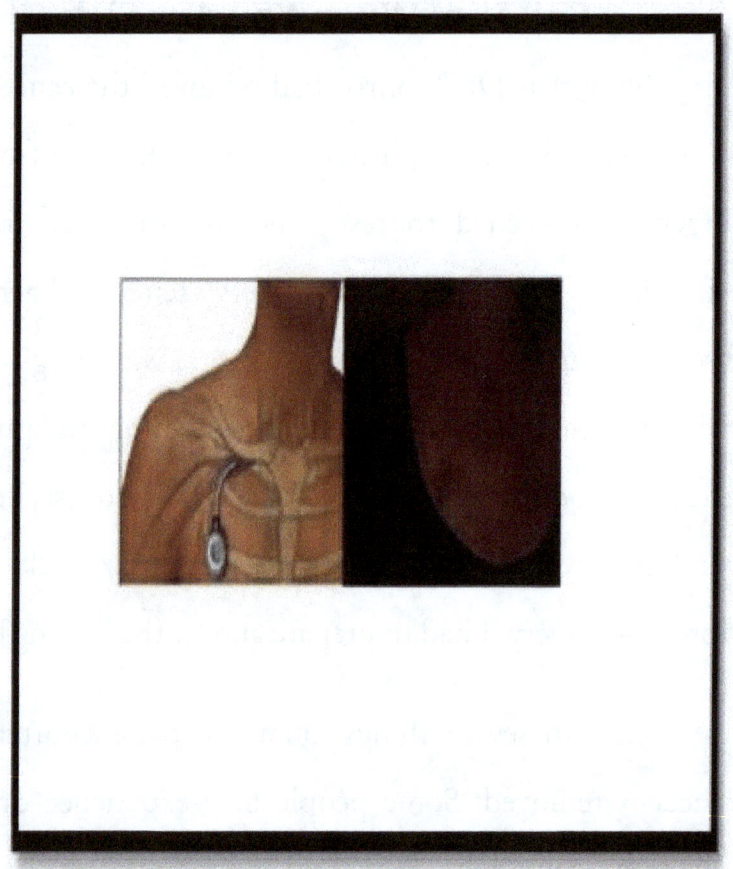

After the cancer was removed, I had to have a catheter, known as a port-a-cath. This port was inserted in my chest during an outpatient surgery with Dr. Monroe. A port is a small disc about the size of a quarter that fits under the skin.

A soft, thin tube called a catheter connects to the port. A nurse inserts the catheter to the port before treatments start and removes it once treatment is completed. The port is used to avoid frequent needle sticks and is given like an Intravenous (IV) Drip. A year after I completed both chemotherapy and radiation treatments, the portacath was surgically removed.

I was provided many books and conversations about what to expect during my recovery. Words cannot express how much I appreciated all of the love that was shown during that season of my life. Singing was helping me pull through. Someone else being able to tell me about what to expect based on their experiences helped me. Some friends sent ladies whom they knew to come to see me. Each of the two women was breast cancer survivors. One survived a mastectomy, and the other survived a lumpectomy. Both women visited me and shared their personal experiences and the different actions that they took to survive. This made my process easier and more believable that I, too, could win the fight against breast cancer.

Stages of Breast Cancer

Stage	Type	Description
0	Non-Invasive	Abnormal cells
I	Invasive	Abnormal cells
II	Invasive	Abnormal cells
III	Invasive	Abnormal cells
IV	Invasive	Metastatic (with spread other parts of the body)

It was time to move to one of the BIGGEST STEPS, which was chemotherapy. Dr. Monroe referred me to Dr. Johnson, the oncologist, for chemotherapy and further treatment. An oncologist is a doctor who provides medical care to people who are diagnosed with cancer using chemotherapy and other medicines. Although I read about chemotherapy, I was anxious to know more outside of what I had already learned. Dr. Johnson had already begun to explain to me the plans for my health before I could even ask the question, *"What is Chemotherapy?"* He made me aware that one should plan to be at the doctor's office for three to four hours for each treatment. He also elaborated on the purpose of chemotherapy, which is to prevent the spread of cancer. Chemotherapy was used to kill the cancer cells in case it had already spread throughout my body. Chemotherapy is one of the biggest steps towards recovery!

Chemotherapy medicines are given through a special needle that fits right into the port. This port is also used to have blood drawn. When I first got the portacath, I could feel it there, but I got used to it after a while. It became like I didn't know it was there because I no longer felt it. I had it for about one year. The port is normally flushed out before and after chemotherapy treatment.

I preferred to get treatments on Mondays because I traveled to sing on the weekends. Once I expressed this to my doctor, my appointments were only scheduled for Mondays. My normal routine time of getting weekly treatments was on Mondays. After I experienced illness, I became an advocate for breast cancer survivors without even knowing it. Naturally, I wanted to uplift men and women who are diagnosed with breast cancer. My message to them is, *"Every day that you can say good morning, you have survived another day. That is reason enough to put on a happy face even when you don't feel like it."* Proverbs 3:13 states, "Happy is the man that findeth wisdom, and the man that getteth understanding." I found reasons to smile. I was so grateful. I chose to fight a good fight of faith despite being diagnosed with breast cancer.

My doctor previously shared with me to expect my hair falling out. My children always knew how much I loved my hair and did not want to lose my hair, but I knew life was more important than hair, clothes, or any physical things. I just wanted to live! I had already prepared myself by purchasing a wig. I can recall going into my daughter's room after my first treatment, and I told her that my hair was coming out. I asked her to wipe my hair out, and she did. Afterwards, I felt some type of way, and I did not feel good about my hair coming out. I remembered that my doctor told me that my hair would return once the chemotherapy treatment was over, so I tried to continue with my day as normal. I had to look beyond the circumstance and thank God for my life. Matthew 6:34 reminds us, "Take therefore no thought for tomorrow: for tomorrow shall take thought for the things of itself." As I reflect on those moments, even that moment, I not only thank God for his strength, but also for the strength that my daughter and son showed towards the circumstance. Both were strong with me and for me.

There were various side effects of having chemotherapy. With each treatment, the side effects made me feel weaker because each time more medicine was being placed in my body. By the second treatment, I had begun experiencing my mouth frequently being parched. I had to keep water with me all of the time. After the third treatment, I was actually able to smell the medicine in my skin. My sense of smell and taste was affected. Other side effects which you may experience are vomiting or diarrhea. While I was already experiencing anemia, I experienced anemia even more during chemotherapy treatments. Anemia is feeling fatigued (very tired), nausea, and a loss of appetite. The oncologist provided me with iron infusions which gave me the energy that I needed after each treatment. Each time chemotherapy would weaken my immune system and I would have to get more iron infusions to build my immune system backup. I have experienced what could have made me feel hopeless, but I knew that there was life beyond my diagnosis. I advocate life and living.

Breast Cancer also has an emotional side effect as you see your illness to be disrupting your life. This type of stress can manifest itself into sleep, fatigue, and tiredness. Of course, it is normal to think about the future. Ecclesiastes 3:1 states, "To everything, there is a season, and a time to every purpose under the heaven;" Know that God is with you and that he is in total control.

God had already ordered my footsteps. He promised never to leave me or forsake me. He promised to be with me even to the end of the earth. Remember, every day that this is the day that the Lord has made. I will rejoice and be glad in it. In other words, God already knows all about you and your circumstances.

Although I did not have an appetite by the fourth treatment, I still tried to eat because I did not want to look sick. I highly disliked the smell of certain scents like hot-dogs, perfumes, or colognes. These scents often made me feel really nauseated. The good news is that for each side effect, the doctors have something to treat it. To maintain good health, it was important that I learned my body.

During the entire process of chemotherapy, I always felt fatigued. Each time I was given an iron infusion treatment to give me a boost, and I felt so much better! Every-time I got a treatment, I had a different side effect. I always felt my best and regained strength once it was near the time for another treatment. There were three weeks scheduled between each treatment. I was still able to sing during my journey of recovery. I know it was God who gave me the strength to travel on the road with my group and attend church. While it was important for me to remain active because I am an outgoing person, it was also necessary for me to rest as much as possible. Because I learned my body, I knew when I felt tired or exhausted.

PERSONAL NOTE: GOD IS STILL THE BEST DOCTOR AND PRAYER IS STILL THE BEST MEDICINE. Try to be positive and let the Lord restore your mind. Philippians 4:8 states, "Finally, brethren, whatsoever things are true, whatsoever things are honest, whatsoever things are just, whatsoever things are pure, whatsoever things are lovely, whatsoever things are of a good report; if there be any virtue, and if there be any praise, think on these things." The scripture teaches us to think positively and remember that laughter is good for the soul! Focus on positive and healing thoughts.

Have you ever heard, "*We are what we eat!*" My experiences taught me that this saying is true. While some people will only have an appetite for certain foods, a balanced diet is essential to building a strong and healthy immune system. Eat more vegetables and fruits whenever you have an appetite. Choose foods that are packed with calories and proteins (protein shake). Drink plenty of fluids, especially on days when you cannot eat. Do not worry when you cannot eat. Just keep track and let your doctor know if your appetite fails to improve within a couple of days. For some people, the best time to eat may be in the morning. For others, it may be noon or night. I maintained a healthy diet by drinking distilled water, green teas, and staying away from red meats. I tried to eat more fruits and vegetables.

Although I was eating healthy, I always referred to what my doctor initially shared with me about the state of one's mind. I focused on positive thoughts as often as I could. Mechanisms I used to fight the circumstance were healthy eating, positive thoughts, and building faith in God through prayers, scriptures, and singing. By my fifth treatment, my fingernails and toenails turned black. I experienced mouth sores. To see your body experience so many physical changes can become a burden. It is important to know when to digress or debrief from thinking about your health status.

For example, during my six months of chemotherapy, I had to get out of the house. I needed to keep myself busy. On days that I felt like doing so, I would often take short walks around my community. I was able to notice the beautiful landscape and flowers in other people's yards. My walks provided intimate time with the Lord and an admiration for nature. I developed inspiration and began to landscape my yard. I decorated my yard with beautiful rocks, Monkey Grass, and Elephant Ears. While I did not have the energy to plant all of these plants alone, I had someone to plant yellow and pink Four O' Clocks and Rose Bushes for me while I supervised. Doing something that you enjoy will relieve you from feeling pain and anxiety. Try to relax. Try distressing yourself with something you like to do. Know that laughter is good. Enjoying family, comedy, or television shows will distress you.

During the time that I received the sixth chemotherapy treatment, I was so happy to know that this journey was almost over although my tongue was black, my skin was darkened, and my hair was out! I was exhausted and fatigued. Yes, this was my final treatment, but it would take much time to recover as the medicine was still in my body. I not only knew but also felt that while I was on a journey to recovery, my body was not the same. My tongue, nails and skin remained dark for some time. In life, we face difficult situations that leave us not knowing what to do or say. Despite what I physically experienced, I knew that my breakthrough had arrived!

God allowed me to go through each of life's challenging moments, so I could encourage others who are going through the same thing. I carry a message, and it is, "*If God brings you to the storm, he will take you through the storm. Whatever you go through, he is there with you. No matter how bad the situation may be. He did it for me; He will do it for you. Your miracle is just right around the corner.*" Psalm 27:14 states, "*Be of good courage and he shall strengthen thine heart. Wait on the Lord*!"

Several years later, my baby brother, Steven reminded me of the encounter that my mother had with the Lord. As I was going through my storm, God was with me. My mother was on this journey with me every step of the way and she often prayed for my health. One Sunday, the group traveled out of town to sing in St. Louis, Missouri. During this service, my mother was just praising God not only for my healing but for him just being God. After her encounter with the Lord that day, my mom said to me, "*I heard him. The Lord told me that you are going to be healed. You are goanna be all right.*" Once she shared her encounter with me and the Word that God spoke to her, she confirmed what I had already felt. I could not help but to give God the highest praise. All I could say was, *"Hallelujah."* I knew that was confirmation for me that I was being healed that moment.

I knew and felt that God had already won my case. I believed that in that moment, I was healed. We first have to believe. Lyrics to one of my mother's favorite songs are, "*God don't answer prayer just the way we want him to. He has us to know that there is something we must do. Call him when you are sick, trouble in mind. He is never late. He steps in on time, and I know he works that way. Yes, I know he works that way.*"

Our experiences we encounter in life will always be for the endurance of someone else. Each burden we bare, each painful encounter we have not only made us stronger to fight the fight of faith but also will bless someone else. I encourage you to be patient. I believe for you that this too shall pass!!! Stay on the course, and do not quit. Stand still and wait on the Lord. I'm in belief that you will survive! Ecclesiastes 9:11 teaches, "The race is not given to the swift, nor the strong but to those who endure to the end." Do not dwell on negative thoughts, guard your heart with all diligence, and fill it with the word of God. Keep filling your heart with the promises of God. I knew that I could do all things through Christ who strengthens me, and you can too!

I would say, for me, Chemotherapy was the hardest part of my journey dealing with breast cancer. I lost my hair. One thing that changed is that I was no longer able to use a relaxer. It took a while for my hair to grow back. After my hair grew back, I thought I could return to relaxing my hair. I found out that I could not because each time I tried my hair came out. Based on the texture of your hair, your hair may not be able to process chemicals the same. Once your hair grows back, you may not be able to relax it anymore.

Recap: As discussed in this chapter, there are various side effects to chemotherapy. Treatments caused me to feel so tired, weak, and nauseated. Usually, most of the time after receiving chemotherapy, you do not feel well. Sometimes there is a delayed reaction, and you begin to feel better just before the next treatment. Because chemotherapy kills good and bad cells, your body will not feel the same. Cells have to regenerate, and recovery takes time. It took my body a while to recover. I would say take your time, laugh as much as you can and surround yourself with loved ones to keep your strength up. Stay focused and know that you are not fighting the battle by yourself. **POSITIVE NOTE: KNOW, THAT THIS TOO SHALL PASS.** Thank God for each day and do all that you can to survive. Know that you are not alone. Keep your head up! This is a process, but God will condition you to overcome.

Chapter 5:
You Can Make It
Play The Hand That You Are Dealt

Here we go! I have a new doctor again! It is time for my first appointment with my radiologist, Dr. Dearny. As I walked in, I began to look around. I asked myself, *"What about this radiation? What are they goanna do to me now?"* Before treatment, I was not as knowledgeable, but I understood the process after experiencing radiation therapy treatment. Radiation is like a bright light bulb shining on the specific area in which cancer was once developed. This light is made of Ultraviolet (UV) waves. These waves are focused on the specific area instead of your entire body. Treatment varies based on the cancer type and location of the cancer. Radiation waves are transferred through the UV. For me, my specific area was the breast.

While experiencing the process, I learned that chemotherapy is required for the whole body because cancer may have spread anywhere. However, radiation is for the specific area in which the cancer was discovered. Radiation kills cancer cells. During my first appointment, the doctor went over various explanations with me. She explained the process of radiation therapy treatments, how long each treatment would last, and the side effects. The longest I ever stayed for a radiation appointment was the first few times, and the last few times I went to the office. The side affects you may have, depends on how much radiation you may receive during your treatments.

During the second appointment, the doctors marked my body with a marker to show where the UV rays would be directed for radiation therapy treatment. The marked area remained throughout the treatments. Wherever the specific area is located, the doctors placed a light to shine on that area to stop cancer cells' growth. I had many treatments, and some days I felt lightheaded and weak. Side effects of radiation can vary from person to person. Radiation does not hurt. My treatments were ongoing. I went for seven weeks. I had thirty-four treatments that were given Monday through Friday. It is important to remember that every person reacts differently to radiation therapy treatments. What you can do depends on how you feel. Some days, I was weaker than others. I was more independent during radiation than I was during chemotherapy. I was able to drive myself and sometimes run a few errands if I felt like it.

My faith was strong, but I reflected on how I never experienced sickness until I was diagnosed with breast cancer. I not only had chemotherapy but also, I had to undergo radiation. There is a saying that I always say, which is, "*You have to play the hand that you are dealt to survive.*" You may ask, "*What do I mean by play?*" Knowledge is power. Learn all that you can about how to deal with the battle you are facing to survive. I had to believe that God was going to help me to get through each circumstance. I really, really leaned on the Lord; I trusted him in the place that I was in. I had to encourage myself, and I did. Leaning and depending on God made me stronger in knowing that I could make it. My doctor once said to me, "*I wish all of my patients were like you.*" I said to him, "*I do not want to pray and worry too.*" I knew I had to keep my mind on the Lord, and put all of my trust in him.

If I had never experienced knowing Jesus, and believing the things that he has already done, I probably would have lost my mind. I always say, *"I have to pray until something happens."* I believed in Jesus, and my faith kept me praying. Mark 5:42 details the story about a child, a girl who was only twelve years old. Jarius was an official and begged Jesus to come and heal his daughter. Jesus did not make haste to go. A bystander in the crowd said to Jarius to leave the crowd and to no longer bother Jesus. However, Jesus paid no attention to the naysayers. Instead, Jesus encouraged Jarius ONLY to BELIEVE. Jesus went by Jarius' home and heard a commotion. The noise was Jarius, who was crying and yelling. Jesus saw Jarius' situation differently than anyone in Jarius' home.

Jarius did what Jesus asked him to do, and that is ONLY to BELIEVE. **PERSONAL NOTE: LIKE JAIRUS, WE TOO MUST ONLY BELIEVE.** You may wonder, *"What do I need to believe?"* You should trust God because trusting is believing. Believe that God is a healer. Believe in what you pray and believe that he would get you through any circumstance. Many times, we hear the word of God, but we fail to listen. Here are five things to help you:

- Hear the word of God.

- Listen to the word of God.

- Allow the word of God to take root (let it grow).

- Ask the Holy Spirit to come into your heart.

- Pray a prayer to ask the Holy Spirit to control your thoughts.

"*Whose report will you believe?*" Yes, sickness is here on earth, but there is no sickness that God cannot heal. 1st John 5:14 states, "And this is the confidence that we have in him, that, if we ask anything according to his will, he heareth us;" The key is we have to pray, and our prayer must be in God's will. 3rd John 1:2 reminds us that God's will is for us to prosper and be in good health. The Bible shares ongoing testimonials of God's response to prayer. Our faith moves God! He did it back then, and he could do it again. While, rarely, we meet believers who believe in God's miraculous works, believing is a requirement from God. We must believe if we are going to please him. Hebrews 11: 6, "But without faith, it is impossible to please him: for he that cometh to God must believe that he is and that he is a rewarder of them that diligently seek him." Even during our current times, as Christians, we must keep faith in God. Keep looking to God. During wars, COVID-19 pandemic, racism, and the many evils of this world, look to God. Always trust God.

The only type of fear that we should have is our fear of God, and the type of fear that promotes good behavior. This is a Godly fear. However, fear can also be a feeling that prevents us from trusting in God. We should never fear to trust God because he knows what is best for us. **PERSONAL NOTE: DO NOT FEAR TO TRUST GOD WITH ANYTHING REGARDLESS OF IF IT IS A BIG OR SMALL CIRCUMSTANCE.** Many people tried to place fear in me while I was going through treatments. Someone said to me, *"Oh, girl, they're goanna open you up, and cancer will spread over your body."* Although someone spoke those words to me, you need to know that in my case this was not true. These words could have terrified me and caused me to fear treatment. I knew what I was told was not true. I did not buy into the spirit of fear. Faith and fear cannot and will not abide together. Beloved, you must choose one. Just as light and dark cannot abide together, faith and fear will not mix. Without a second thought, I chose faith. For anyone making personal choices, I will tell you that God will guide you. If it is not of God, he will let you know.

I say unto you today, my sister and my brother, "*Do all you can to win. That means to do all that you can to survive.*" Whatever circumstances you encounter, God will carry you through. I recall that once I went to the doctor, and while waiting in the lobby, I was holding a conversation with a woman. I told her, "*If God brings you to it, he can take you through it even the toughest moments of your life. Just do all that you can, and let God do the rest.*" For example, being sick, family crisis, financial instability, or whatever circumstance you are experiencing, God will bring you through. While I am here, I will live and keep my eyes on the prize. Who is the prize? His name is Jesus.

God has a way of teaching us that we are not in control of situations that may occur. However, we can control our spirits and make sure that we have God's fruits within us. Galatians 5:22-23 states, "But the fruit of the spirit is love, joy, peace, forbearance, kindness, goodness, faithfulness, gentleness, and self-control. Against such things, there is no law." As I experienced these circumstances, I made sure I kept love, faith, and hope. I could not see any further than the current day, but what I could do on any given day and at any given moment is hope. So, what I say to you is take one day at a time, and never give up hope.

I remember driving myself to radiation treatment, and on the way home, I said, *"Okay, God, I have gone through this day now take me through the next."* I would say to anyone who may need encouragement, *"Despite what you are going through, do not let the devil put thoughts in your mind."* Do not dwell on the negative. Dwell on the positive. Eternal life is the reward for those whose mind is stayed on Christ Jesus.

I made it this far by trusting in God and singing songs of Zion. Singing, shopping, and walking were all types of therapy for me. The word teaches in Nehemiah 8:10b, "Do not grieve, for the Lord's joy is your strength." If you can get a scripture and a song in your heart, it will get you through anything. "*God's Got Everything You Need*" was one of the songs I often felt and still feel so much joy when I sing. God is the only one who can strengthen us. He holds the whole world in his hands, and you and I. Whenever you feel weak, or as if the future is unknown, trust in God.

I remembered a song that I wrote, *"Lord, If You Guide Me, I Will Not Go Wrong."* This song says, *"You said you would guide me. I am looking to you, Lord."* Proverbs 3:5-7 states, "Trust in the Lord with all thine heart and lean not to thine own understanding. In all thy ways acknowledge him and he shall direct thy path." Because I knew what I was experiencing, this song often restored my faith. This song resonated with me because of my circumstance. I often thanked God in advance for healing me.

Recap: Most people do not know what it is like to have breast cancer nor do they understand the significance of it. We should educate ourselves as much as we can whenever we are diagnosed with breast cancer or any illness. The dosage of radiation that you may receive is determined by your doctor. As mentioned in this chapter, radiation has many side effects. Radiation leaves your body little by little. The most common side effect is that you may feel fatigue during treatments. Your skin may appear to be darker after radiation. Radiation and chemotherapy can cause tooth decay.

Sharp pains may follow treatments. For example, many years after receiving radiation, I still experience sharp pains in my breast. Despite how you may feel, keep your mind on Jesus. Remember that in moments when life is darkest, Jesus will be your light. A scripture and a song in your heart will get you through these tough times. While the journey to recover may seem to take over your whole life, it is important to keep your mind on the future as radiation will only be for a period of time. Allow yourself time to adjust to your circumstance, and to accept the physical and emotional changes. Do not allow pressure to cause you to resume too soon to daily tasks. Keep your mind on the future for this only a process.

Chapter 6:
Wait On The Lord To Move
The State of Mind

As I continued my journey with radiation, I was hopeful because of the thoughts in my mind. Romans 12:2 states, "Do not be conformed to this world but be transformed by the renewing of your mind." **PERSONAL NOTE: GOD IS A KEEPER!** Lord, I am so glad that you kept my mind through all that I have experienced and endured. Through it all, I know that God is carrying me. Despite your ability to sing, preach, or teach about the goodness of Jesus every day, we still have to face the storms of life, and trouble will come. Trouble will weaken your spirit. Sometimes trouble will be so big that you have to reach and get someone to help you pray! During this time, you have to get up from being knocked down and refocus. I thank God for my state of mind even to this date.

Going through my next stages of radiation, I still remembered that it is all in the state of your mind. During my initial diagnosis, I did not want to discuss my illness or be a part of any conversations. After a few years, I began to speak up. I told my story to everyone I met. Rather I am walking in the park or standing in the grocery store line, I love to share my story. I want people to know what God what has done for me. I was really grateful that God had spared my life. I had to align my mind with the word of God as in Jeremiah 29:11, "For I know the plans I have for you," declares the LORD, "plans to prosper you and not to harm you, plans to give you hope and a future." God's word made me feel overjoyed and compassionate to the extent that I wanted to share my testimony with all of the people whom I came in contact.

Once I began to use my voice regarding breast cancer awareness, I never stopped. God placed it in my heart to go through with treatment. If someone told me something negative, I never accepted it. I tried to always speak positively concerning the situation, and not to let my mind be weighed down by worrying or thinking too much about the negative words that someone said because I know the God I serve. I often asked myself, "*How can I worry about it if I am going to pray about it?"* I choose to conform to the word of God by speaking the word at all times. Proverbs 23:7 states, "For as a man thinketh in his heart, so is he."

If you are having a down moment or not in a happy place in your mind, you need to know that God is in control. Read Psalm 23, which states, "The Lord is my shepherd; I shall not want. He maketh me to lie down in green pastures: he leadeth me beside the still waters. He restoreth my soul: he leadeth me in the paths of righteousness for his name's sake. Yea, though I walk through the valley of the shadow of death, I will fear no evil: for thou art with me; thy rod and thy staff they comfort me. Thou preparest a table before me in the presence of mine enemies: thou anointest my head with oil; my cup runneth over. **"Surely goodness and mercy shall follow me all the days of my life and I will dwell in the house of the Lord."** This scripture is one that I use as seeds of wisdom and encouragement. I often say this Psalm as a prayer. Psalm 23:1-2 helps calm anxieties and fears. Psalm 91 is also a scripture of protection and can be used as a seed of wisdom. This scripture is also a send go. Meaning, whenever you cannot physically reach a loved one, you can use Psalm 91 and send a prayer for strength. Psalm 91 is pure in the thought that God will give His angels charge over us despite wars, sickness, and even illness. This is what Jesus Christ does; he sends his angels to camp around us. Although we cannot see the angels, we have to rely on our faith. Psalm 91 is a comforting passage.

PERSONAL NOTE: GOD WILL GIVE HIS ANGELS CHARGE OVER US! Psalm 91:6 has one key verse that appeals the most to me, and it states, "Nor for the pestilence that walketh in darkness; nor for the destruction that wasteth at noonday." You may ask, *"What is a pestilence?"* A pestilence is an infectious, fatal disease that is widespread or an evil influence. Therefore, we know that Covid-19 is a pestilence. Cancer is a pestilence. There are many pestilences in today's world. This passage is a prayer for protection against pestilences such as Covid- 19, cancer, plagues, diseases, illnesses, and demonic forces. Despite what you are going through or others, continue to pray for a hedge of protection from God. God is our refuge (the one we rely on) when we are going through the storms of life. Our experiences of going through must be one day at a time.

Recap: If you are seeking peace during a crisis, know that you can pray and ask God for his gift of the Holy Spirit to comfort you despite what you are going through. The heaviness of seeing my body change as I experienced chemotherapy and radiation, was a burden that only the Holy Spirit could have carried for me. Whenever your load is too heavy to bare, remember that God is in control. Despite what occurs in our lives, God has a plan to help us get through it. God can make possible what man feels is in impossible.

As my body experienced chemotherapy and radiation, I often prayed for God's protection while focusing on seeds of wisdom. There were moments when I had to refocus my attention on Jesus because my heart and my mind was heavy. It is important to fix our thoughts when we are challenged with the pestilences of today's world. We must rely on the Holy Spirit to strengthen our hearts and minds to help us to overcome. God is a healer even of our thoughts!

Chapter 7:

Have A Little Talk With Jesus

He Is Strong When You Are Weak

I was down to the end of my radiation therapy treatments. Although I had thirty-four treatments, and I thought I was at the end, thirty-four treatments were not quite the end. There is always a continuation of doctor visits required for one to continue taking care of their health. Now, I am prepared to begin wrapping up radiation appointments and continue with taking care of my health through frequent check-ups and doctor visits. Whenever I felt strong enough, I did my best to get up and get dressed. I always told people, *"I was not sick; I was just going through the motions."* Doing this taught me that I am healed, and I overcame by the words of my testimony. **PERSONAL NOTE: YOU, TOO, CAN OVERCOME!**

There are various side effects one may experience with radiation therapy treatment. During this period, I continued to eat foods that built my immune system to be the strongest it can be, and I tried to drink plenty of water. Sometimes drinking plenty of water can be hard. Water is important to everyone, regardless of if a person is experiencing treatments or not. I continued to flush my body with water and lemons because the medicine is strong. The main short-term side effects are swelling, vomiting, hair loss, redness or soreness of the breast, skin changes in areas similar to a sunburn, tenderness of the skin, and tooth decay.

Some of the side effects that I experienced were feeling fatigued and tired. One morning, after twenty-seven treatments or so I woke up and I had clear blisters all over my breast. I reported it to the doctors. The radiation began to burn my skin. No worries, hunny! The doctors gave me some crème for my burning that was so powerful, and it cleared it up in a few days. I thought that the doctors would have stopped treatments, but they continued. Regardless of what side affects you may experience; no side effects are too small to report. If you experience any side effects, let your physician know. Once you have reported your side effects, your physician will take care of you.

At the completion of radiation therapy, my body had to heal. I actually still have the discoloration from the radiation. A person needs to have a good support system during these times. If someone offers to pray for you or do any good deed to be a blessing, let them be a blessing. There is a saying that I once heard when I was a child that says, *"You do not need nobody but Jesus."* This is not true. Jesus works through people. He placed people here to help you. Let them help you. **PERSONAL NOTE: LET FAMILY HELP YOU! YOU SHALL HAVE HELP (1st Samuel 1:9).**

As I have mentioned, make good food choices. Once treatment has ended, and you become strong enough, it is also essential to keep your body as active as you can, pray without ceasing, and give thanks in all circumstances. Try to eat at least two to three servings of fruits and vegetables each day and do some form of exercise for thirty minutes at least three times a week. For example, walking is a good exercise, and it is free. While you may feel too busy, it is important to make time for yourself. Be cautious about what you put in your body. If you decide to eat anything that is not healthy, then eat it in moderation. Begin to speak life to yourself and tell yourself, *"I can do it!"* Boost your health by eating healthy foods. The Bible ongoingly teaches about healthy foods. Deuteronomy 8:8 describes a land that God had promised his people, "A land of wheat and barley, of vines and fig trees and pomegranates, a land of olive oil and honey;" These are the foods that God promised us so that our bodies can be in the best condition and in good health. There are various Biblical references to the types of foods that are most healthy. Have you ever heard the saying, *"An apple a day keeps the doctor away?"* Apples are heart-healthy! In general, foods with the most color – dark green, red, yellow, and orange – have the most nutrients.

Changing our lifestyles as far as what we eat can help us in many ways. You are what you eat! Fruits and vegetables are good for your bones. For example, the book of Daniel tells the story about three Hebrew Boys Hananiah, Mishael, and Azariah (later named Shadrach, Meshach, and Abednego). Daniel 1:16 states, "So the guard took away their choice food and the wine they were to drink and gave them pulse instead."

Pulse is a Biblical reference for vegetables such as legumes, lentils, chickpeas, and any seed type of food. The point of the story is that the Hebrew Boy's appearance looked better based on the type of foods they consumed.

The Bible provides many references to what we should eat. Numbers 11:5 states, "We remember the fish we ate in Egypt at no cost-also the cucumbers, melons, leeks, onions, and garlic;" This scripture provides us with a list of foods that are Biblical. Put in your all to be as healthy, whole, and well as you can be. Build your body up by resting. Take each day that you are given as a blessing from the Lord. If you know of anyone who is experiencing any type of cancer or illness, always strive to make them feel loved and important. Put all that you experience in the Lord's hands. It is essential in the Body of Christ that we build ourselves and others up.

Recap: Start by making small changes to your diet. Water not only makes up most of your body weight, but also flushes out toxins from your body. We should make healthy food choices. Remember, God wants us to take steps to be as healthy and whole as we can be.

Chapter 8:
God Kept His Arms Around Me
Pulling Me Through

Keeping building! Do not allow life's circumstances to tear you down. If you feel too weak to go on, remember God's strength is made perfect in your weakness. For example, God made me strong when I was weak (Romans 12:9). God pushes me, and I pushed myself. After chemotherapy and radiation therapy treatment, my body was really weak. It took a higher power to build me up. That power is the power of God's Holy Spirit. Philippians 4:13 states, "I can do all things through Christ which strengthens me." You should always feed your mind with God's word. I experienced doing so, and I know that this will build you up!

Because of the responsibility of keeping up with doctor visits, taking care of family, or even everyday duties, anyone feeling weak should always build their spirits up. Building ourselves up begins with God's Word. The most important thing to remember is for you to work hard and do all that you can do but know that Jesus Christ's strength is made perfect in your weakness. I tried to always encourage myself, no matter what I encountered. I say to men, women, young boys and girls, *"Prayer is essential. If you have prayed about it and trust in God, he will be with you. In the time of trouble, God is a very present help. Tell God to guide the way. He said he would."*

I had to trust God. God's Holy Spirit not only kept me encouraged but also allowed me to encourage others. I was able to share my story with someone I met at the community center. After I told her about my experience, she told me what was going on with her. I asked her to go out to breakfast so that we can talk. Once she and I began to speak, I shared with her the importance of going to the doctor and doing what the doctor said. This lady was newly diagnosed. She caught the cancer in time. After she and I spoke, she felt better about having surgery. Cancer was removed from her body, and she only had to have radiation. In the midst of my storm, I tried to encourage others with the Word of God. I kept reminding myself that all things would work together for my good. It is important to speak life to others.

PERSONAL NOTE: THIS IS JUST A PROCESS, AND YOU WILL COME OUT. Shake off the fear and look at your vision. This is just a set up for a comeback! See yourself coming out beautiful. See yourself celebrating life. See yourself healthy. See yourself living your best life. See yourself saying, "*I am cancer free.*" See yourself as a survivor. See yourself going on vacation. See yourself telling someone, "*I made it out.*" See yourself telling your friends and family, "*I feel great!*" See yourself saying, look where God brought me from. Look through your eyes of faith and see yourself healed. See yourself having peace of mind. See yourself winning the battle.

Recap: Keep the future in mind! Your future is bright! Be patient as you recover! A lot of times illness, and disease cause fears. We become uneasy and worry. It is not at all easy all to deal with breast cancer or any type of illness. Pray, pray, and pray because fear deals with the mind. Keep praying until you overcome. The best prescription is to pray until something happens.

Chapter 9:
God Can Do It
This Too Shall Pass

God can do anything except fail. I ask you to believe that God can heal your body, mind and soul. For example, although my encounter was some time ago, I always knew that God could heal me. My faith kept me believing that any current problems will pass, and brighter days were ahead. I recall being in a circumstance where my health insurance ended after my treatments were done. I knew God was able to provide for me. As a result of my faith, I was told about a five-year program that I could utilize. This program helped me and I was able to continue all of my doctor visits.

If you need insurance or coverage after you have been diagnosed, I encourage you to consult with your local health department to review resources that maybe available to you. Also, there may be assistance through your community clinic through various programs. At the completion of chemo and radiation therapy treatment, I still had many follow-up appointments, and I had to have medicine. Having my health care expenses covered brought me hope and taught me that there are resources for those who may not be insured while battling with cancer and are in need of medical treatment.

Going through treatments as you recover can feel overwhelming. The doctors will give you a lot of information during your treatments. Having a notepad, or being able to record the information that your doctor is telling you is helpful. I mentioned early on that knowledge is power. Learn about your condition and what you can do to help yourself. **PERSONAL NOTE: CHARTING DETAILS WILL PREPARE YOU FOR HOW TO HELP YOU TAKE CARE OF YOUR HEALTH NEEDS.**

Even if you have completed breast cancer treatment, the doctors still need to watch you closely. It is very important to go to all of your follow-up appointments. **PERSONAL NOTE: NEVER GET TO A POINT WHERE YOU STOP GOING TO THE DOCTOR.** After being diagnosed with any type of cancer, you should never stop going to your follow-up appointments to report any changes that is in your body no matter how small. During these visits, your doctor will ask if you have any problems and run your blood work to ensure that all of your counts are normal. A complete blood count is a blood test used to evaluate your overall health. Your doctor will determine and make you aware of how often you should have a blood test.

My follow up visits initially were scheduled for once a month. After some time, I began to go quarterly, then once every six months. The longer you have been free of cancer, the less appointments are needed. Although you are scheduled once a year with your oncologist, you should keep up with your primary doctor at a minimum of at least one visit per six months. If you not only keep up with your primary doctor visits, but also your oncologist, any changes in your health will be detected sooner than later. Although it is a lot of work, be persistent in making all of your doctor visits.

Years later, my follow-up appointment with my oncologist is still once a year. You may be required to have numerous testing after completion of radiation therapy treatment. The goal of follow-up care is to make sure that there is no recurrence of cancer. The main thing you should know is that the doctors will take care of you.

A key scripture I often referred to is Isaiah 41:10, which states, "Fear not, for I am with you; Be not dismayed, for I am your God. I will strengthen you. Yes, I will help you; I will uphold you with My righteous right hand." God's word was always food to my soul, even during my long ten years of taking medicine.

Tamoxifen was one of the medicines that I took ongoing for ten years. Tamoxifen prevents estrogen from helping cancer cells grow and is used to prevent breast cancer among women who are at a high risk. Be aware that this medicine may have side effects. I experienced hot flashes and body aches. Tamoxifen is the first hormonal therapy to be used during the first five years of treatment. A woman's menopause status will determine hormonal treatment for the second five years. Drugs used to treat breast cancer are considered systemic therapies. It's often used to reduce the risk of cancer recurrence in women who have been treated for early-stage breast cancer. The continuation of taking medicine is based on your doctor's recommendation, and your menopause status. I would advise anyone to take the prescriptions, follow your doctor's medical advice, and trust God. Never give in to fear. Be ready for a fight! The doctors are there to take care of you when you follow up and keep going, especially if something seems irregular. We have to do our part and make sure that we are going to the doctor and being attentive to our bodies. Doctor visits are never over! You have to take charge of your health! Fight for good health! In my experiences, I have learned to share with family members to be aware of their bodies' changes. Do not be afraid to reach out to other people and communicate about your experiences to help others. **PERSONAL NOTE: START DISCUSSING HEALTH MATTERS EARLY IN LIFE.** Rather you are talking to a sister, niece, aunt, or close friend, discuss important health matters. Many times, we fail to share personal details about our health. However, one in eight women will have breast cancer in their lifetimes.

Because of such statistics, early detection is our best protection. Share with those whom you love. Never hesitate to provide them with knowledge or experience you may have that pertains to breast cancer. During everyday encounters and conversations, anyone can advocate. As women, we often take care of everybody, and we put ourselves last. But if you do not take care of you, you will not be able to take care of anybody else!

Here are some tips for you to share whenever you are advocating about breast cancer:

1. Pay close attention to your body. Whenever something looks or feels different, get check.

2. Genetic testing is important. If there is a number of people who have gotten diagnosed in your family, you should get tested.

3. If someone does not have health insurance, they can call to their local health department or their community clinic to find out information. Breast and Cervical Programs are available for screening.

Although sometimes, a person may not have any symptoms or warning signs, the most common symptoms are as follows:

1. Breast pains

2. Lump (s)

3. Hard mass or irregular masses

4. Swelling on all or part of the breast

5. Breast or nipple pain

6. Nipple discharge

7. Nipple or breast skin that is red, dry, flaking, or thickening.

8. Swelling lymph nodes under the arm or around the collar bone.

9. Skin dimpling.

Throughout this book, we have discussed the importance of prayer. Always do the best you can to be in good health and never doubt that God wants what is best for you. The word of God states in 1st Peter 4:8, "Beloved, I wish above all things that you may prosper and be in health, even as your soul prospers;" God wants what is best for us. We know what to do and how to do it best whenever we surround ourselves with those who can teach us. If you do not have the information that you need, learn where to find it. Make conversations about health just as we talk about food, restaurants, parties, and television shows. A person does not have to be a breast cancer survivor to be an advocate for breast cancer.

Recap: Health awareness should begin among young children at the age of thirteen. We should teach our children to recognize changes in their body as it may regard any type of illness. As we have stated throughout this book, "*Early detection is the best protection.*" Learn to have regular examinations and teach your family and friends to the same also. Having a Pap Smear is beneficial because it will allow the doctors to determine if something is different. You should have a Pap Smear every one to two years.

Chapter 10

How We Made It

Trusting And Believing

Being diagnosed with breast cancer is not the end of the world. I have been blessed to be a part of many different support groups. Being involved with support groups and engaging with others has been comforting. I have been blessed to be around women who have gone through similar experiences as me. I have learned so much by being in support groups. Various people from all walks of life have gone through having been diagnosed with breast cancer and survived. Throughout this book, many stories have been shared, which will resonate with you to bring hope and understanding. Despite what you experience, you can make it.

Pray this prayer with me:

"Lord, I trust you. Father you are a great God! You are the great Father. I know you want me to be healthy. I know that you want me to be healed, so I decree, and I declare. I speak *over every part of my body that I will live without cancer, without pain, without hurt and without stress. You said in your word, that you would be with me even until the end of the earth, so I know that you are here with me during this time of my life, and I speak healing right now in your name, Amen."*

The following testimonials are provided to express the importance of self-care and how essential it is to be consistent with going to the doctor. Here are some testimonials to encourage you to let you know that you are not alone in your walk. Fight to survive!

Testimony # 1

"Where do I begin? At some point in my life, I always knew sickness would come such as arthritis, high blood pressure, or maybe a common cold, but never ever did I think of Breast Cancer. My diagnosis was discovered during my annual mammogram check-up in April 2015, Stage 2. Needless to say, the news shook me and my family's very foundation.

Once office meetings and lab testing were done, my surgery was scheduled to remove the mass on April 21, 2015. Two weeks after my surgery, I began chemotherapy. My oncologist assured me that my hair would come out. So, my husband suggested that if I were going to lose my hair, we would shave it before the chemotherapy took it out. He shaved my hair. He was crying, and I was also. In support of me, my daughter cut her hair off. My pastor told me to recover quickly. I wore stylish wigs and head wraps. By my second chemotherapy treatment, my head was completely bald. My self-esteem was in question, but I had to keep telling myself that God saved my life, and I was soooo grateful. I had four months of chemotherapy and thirty-three treatments of radiation. I am here to tell my story, and I am soooo very grateful to God, my healer. I had all of the love and support from my family and church family. I pray that my journey will help someone during their test. May God bless and keep you. I owe God."

Kim Love
5 Year Survivor

Testimony # 2

"I am ninety years old, and I am a thirty-year breast cancer survivor. I find that we are what we eat. I encourage anyone who is diagnosed with breast cancer to get some information on healthy eating. One of the things you can look at is not going on a strict diet but just cut back on what you are eating that is unhealthy such as salt, grease, or sugars. You can have whatever you want sometimes, but you cannot have it all of the time. Do portion control. Portion control will help you a lot.

Exercise. My exercise is walking. Have a partner. If you do not have a partner, you may not do it. Many women use many different methods of coping after treatment. Some women join a support group. When you get in a support group, you get to hear other women's stories, and you get to share any problems you are having. You can get a list of support groups from the American Cancer Society.

Carefully read your information over and over again. Knowledge is power! You need to feel like, I am going to cope with this. Whatever you do, do not isolate yourself. If you do, you may end up needing emotional or mental support. Remember, when you look good, you feel good."

Audrey L.

30 Year Survivor

Testimony #3

"Do all you can to save your life."

Judy T.

25 Year Survivor

Testimony #4

"I am eighty-three years old, and I have gone to God many times in prayer. Trust in God and know that God is a healer. He says we have not because we ask not. If we ask him to heal our bodies, he will do according to his will. Never say what you cannot do until you try."

Alice T.

14 Year Survivor

Testimony #5

"I am a thirteen-year cancer survivor. God is in control. Whatever you are going through, you must trust in the Lord, and trust in your doctors as well because they know what is best for you."

Katie M.

13 Year Survivor

Testimony #6

"I was diagnosed with Stage 1 Breast Cancer in 2014 and 2018. I am now breast cancer-free with a ten-year oral treatment plan. I am six years and seven months into the treatment, and I have changed medication only once. Whenever a person hears the word cancer, their heart drops. The second time around, I was thinking it has metastasized and started to spread all over my body. That was not true! It was my mind playing tricks on me. The next morning, I was still very sad; however, I heard God say, "Trust me; I got you. Stop crying. Get up and live. Just live." On that day, I got up, and I began to live, trust, and obey God's word. I trust him as he knows what is good for me."

Dorothy T.

6 Year Survivor

Testimony #7

"The most important thing that I found out is that one must have a strong support system. People who have never gone through breast cancer will never understand chemotherapy's side effects or the loneliness that one may feel. A support system helped me. I could not see the forest for the tree. I only saw the now, but my support system kept telling me to see the future. I would tell any man or woman to get into a good support system. Breast cancer is tyranny to men. Most men call it chest cancer; they do not call it breast cancer. There is a lack of awareness among males concerning breast cancer."

Mr. Vance S.

(Three time) 6 Year Survivor

Testimony # 8

Kiesha D. states, her grandmother, "Claudie T. is 86 years old. For three years, she has survived five types of cancer. The cancer has not metastasized in three years. God let them all be still. Some of them have shrunk. Claudie T. is not bothered. She is still cooking for herself and her husband *every day. She is still fighting. Her life, living, and faith is a testimony of what God can do."*

Claudie T.

3 Year Survivor

Testimony #9

"I was devastated when the doctors told me I had breast cancer, and my first thought was about my children. I wondered to myself, "What about them? What about my husband? How long do I have? What am I going to do now?" I cried that night, asking God, "Why me?" The next morning, I understood that God allowed me to be an example. I would tell anyone who is facing news like this to pray and ask God for guidance. He will see you through. I leaned on God because HE is where my strength came from. I know that he is the reason why I am still living and being an example to others by showing that you, too, can win the race. Ask God, and he will go with you through the storm."

Camilla J.

3 Year Survivor

Testimony #10

"On May 26, 2019, I discovered a lump in my right breast from breast evaluation. Long story short, I was diagnosed with BREAST CANCER, and I began the long process of treatments. What can I tell you? When they first called me, I said, "Not, me!" I thought about my teenage daughter and my husband. I began surgeries, CHEMOTHERAPY, and a month-long of radiation. Later my treatments ended at the end of September 2020. Yes, there were numerous doctor appointments, mammograms, and procedures. The Lord delivered me out of them all. He will do the same for you. I utilize a powerful little book, God's Creative Power for Healing, and speaking the Word of God over my body. I began to strengthen my relationship with the Lord Jesus Christ, who began to give me hope that I should live and not die. Eyes have not seen, ears have not heard, I am getting ready to see something I have never seen. It is according to your faith, and he later said there would be glory after this. So please surround yourself with bishops, evangelists, missionaries, and mentors such as Vanessa

Brown-Knowles. I was determined to live. Cancer is just a common cold to God."

Tonya O. L.
1 Year Survivor

Testimony #11

"*I am thirty-nine years old. I did know prior, but the words came to me, "Don't give up." Trust God and hang in there. When you hear the word cancer alone is a scary thing. Having faith in God was the only thing that kept me. I had to believe! I wanted to get through it, and I did.*"

Sophia G.
1 Year Survivor

Testimony # 12

"*They are looking at a testimony. I am a testimony. Do not write out your obituary because you have cancer. You can still live and survive. Profess Psalm 118:17, "I will live and not die to declare the works of the Lord."*"

Jewel H.
3 Years Survivor

Testimony #13

"Everything Will Be Alright. I know your mind is telling you a lot of things right now but listen to me, everything will be alright. This is not the end. There is healing through cancer. There is deliverance through cancer. This journey may not be easy, but in the end, you will be victorious. Whatever you do, do not give up! Fight! In all things, you have to fight for what you want, so do not give up now. Always remember that you are not alone. Lean on your family and friends for support. Do not be afraid to ask questions and remember, you are not alone! Everything will be alright. Trust in the Lord. Philippians 4:13 states, "I can do all things through Christ which strengthens me."

Rosalyn B.
14 Year Survivor

Being Content In The State That I Was In

www.ingramcontent.com/pod-product-compliance
Lightning Source LLC
LaVergne TN
LVHW050625090426
835512LV00007B/678